YOU
CAN
TEACH
— YOUR CHILDREN —

.... AND
FULFILL
THE
GREAT
COMMISSION

R. David Joyce

WESTBOW
PRESS®
A DIVISION OF THOMAS NELSON
& ZONDERVAN

Scripture taken from the King James Version of the Bible.

WestBow Press books may be ordered through booksellers or by contacting:

WestBow Press
A Division of Thomas Nelson & Zondervan
1663 Liberty Drive
Bloomington, IN 47403
www.westbowpress.com
1 (866) 928-1240

ISBN: 978-1-5127-9000-9 (sc)

Print information available on the last page.

WestBow Press rev. date: 08/04/2017

Table of Contents

and...

THE THREE LEVELS OF LEARNING

PART TWO

and...

USEFUL IDEAS

H ave you been blessed by God with a child? I'm sure you watch carefully for evidence of growth and development in several areas. You watch for recognition when you enter their space. You watch for the first time your child sits up, stands, walks, and formulates words. Each small step is exciting! It can also be distressing. Each step of development takes a child, who God has loaned to you, toward independence and out of your care!

Each growth in development, takes a child away from depending on the parent. It seems, sometimes, this will never happen, and then .....it has! The big question we need to ask ourselves is, "Am I purposely focused on using all of my God-given ability to prepare my children for the society they will live in?" The society is obviously in chaos! There is more loneliness, mental illness, drugs, sexual perversion, and suicides, than ever before! It is possible, however, for you to prepare your child for success! What follows are my thoughts, not so much on what worked, but <u>what I wish I had known,</u> about teaching my family as the children grew in our home. I wish I had done a better job preparing them to function in our rapidly changing world.

I believe God has prepared me with insights that could be helpful to others. I was raised in a home with loving parents who put God first. I have been part of several churches and seen how God's people are supposed to relate. My career in teaching took me to classroom and supervisor opportunities at all levels from

Kindergarten to Graduate University. In the church I served as deacon and youth leader. I have also been involved in developing Christian schools and helping home-schoolers.

I would like to share with you the GOOD NEWS – that God knows you and your children better than anyone else! He has already laid out a pathway for each of you! It is a …

Personal,
  Pleasant.
    Prescribed,
      Purpose,
       …..with a Promise!

It is my prayer that whoever reads this will accept God's plan and walk with Him in one hand……… and your child in the other!

❦ *Acknowledgement* ❦

Fifteen years before I was born, my Father used his Saturday afternoons off work, to visit homes in the South East of Toronto. He invited children to a Thursday evening presentation of the Gospel in a rented hall. He was all out for sharing the story of redemption through Jesus Christ to everyone. The year before I was born, he and his friends formed a church and moved into a new building they had constructed. By the time I was old enough to start kindergarten, I met with a dozen or so others for Sunday School. We sat on benches in a tiny kitchen because it was the only space available. By that time, Dad was Superintendent of the Sunday School. He had 35 to 40 teachers and over 300 students. Although not a teacher by training, he met with his teachers in our tiny home at least 4 times a year to teach them. I still have some of his books that emphasized the importance of reaching children through both "ear gate" and "eye gate".

He supported the family by selling industrial machinery, and was well known and respected across the country. In all of this he was home almost every evening for dinner-time. It was his favourite time for teaching the family. I remember one of his many teaching moments. After dinner he arranged all the cups and dishes to represent Jesus with His disciples on the hill near Bethany, 40 days after His resurrection. The salt shaker in the middle represented Jesus. It was carefully lifted up to represent His ascension into heaven just after He had pronounced His Great Commission **to us all**…

"GO... PREACH...TEACH...MAKE DISCIPLES..."

This type of teaching left significant memories in a small boy. It is what I have tried to show through these pages. My earthly father and mother became conduits of our heavenly Father's love. Whatever I have been able to pass on is because of God's message flowing through my words to you. These are not my ideas.

In contrast, the "god of this world" is described as one who would steal your children, through their own desires, to miss out on the life-giving message of redemption. We need to become INTENTIONAL about pointing them to the Saviour, Who is the only "way, the truth, and the life"! Jesus said that we must all come as little children. It has been said that at least half of those who come to Christ, and acknowledge HIM as LORD, do so before they turn twelve. We need to direct them to HIM early!

It is much more difficult later! The world is offered to them by the evil one...like candy-coated poison, ...that is difficult for them to resist! I do believe that as parents we are able to teach our children, which will strengthen the church and the entire body of Christ. We have tended to expect "the church" to do it for us! It has been given to us! One of the saddest verses in Scripture is in Judges 2:10 where it says that after Joshua died the next generation arose that "KNEW NOT GOD"!

It is my prayer that this will not be said of the generation that follows us!

Chapter One

When God took his people out of Egypt, He presented to them, through Moses, His first love message, in the form of words and objects so they would begin to understand Who He was. Then he told them (Deuteronomy 6) that parents were to teach them to their children on a daily basis, when they arose, when they walked together, when they ate together, and when they went to bed. It was to be taught continuously. The entire family was to function in relationship. In recent times we have chosen to ignore God's plan and go with the flow, so to speak. Our children have been handed to others to teach them what the society thinks is best for them. Let's examine what we could be doing, and see if God's model would serve our children better.

God has made each child unique. As we shall see later, the person who knows the children best, has the best opportunity to teach them. The parents obviously can know their children better than anyone else. In fact, mothers know their children best! They have developed a bond that was formed before their birth, and was quickly enriched in the first few days of their lives. Throughout their formative years a mother's bond is built, that is the source of a rich relationship. It has a somewhat different meaning for a daughter than it has for a son. It is, ultimately, a powerful influence on a child's understanding of the physical and the spiritual.

In the physical realm a girl learns what it means to be feminine and how to mother her family later. In the spiritual realm a daughter and son also learn something of the heart of God from their mother, in ways that men cannot express.

They learn the value of relationship and love, so they will be able to function in the roles God has already laid out for them. To her son, a mother also becomes his ideal of a perfect wife – the one he will search for as a life partner. The mother, in accepting her son as a man, begins to build him up to face adult responsibilities by showing respect for his positive character qualities.

A father's bonding begins a little later, but not too much. At birth, the child already knows the sound of father's voice and as the father helps provide contact and provision, the baby begins to bond with him. The father's presence and interaction with the growing child helps develop a full foundation for growth and development. Specifically, a father is the one who can demonstrate to a son what it means to be masculine, and how to recognize himself as a man when he reaches his early teens. The son's positive character traits can be built on, by the father, through the reward of honour and respect. To his daughter, Dad becomes her vision of an ideal man – the one she will wait for and marry. In the spiritual realm, father's most important role is to demonstrate on a day-to-day basis, as many of the attributes of God, that he can provide.

God expects us parents to do our absolute best to emulate the nature of God to our children on a day-by-day basis! Such an ideal needs to be taken seriously with the knowledge that we are not expected to perform this perfectly or on our own strength! Over and over in scripture the attributes of God are compared to, and illustrated by, family relationships. A healthy family is often the starting point for a son or daughter finding God. This could be seen as an impossible task if we were expected to do it on our own. However, with our hand in God's, we need to begin. With daily prayer and commitment, God will work wonders through us. It is God's program, and He knows us and our children far better than we do. He also knows that when we are committed to doing His work His way, we will be blessed beyond measure! When Jesus was asked for the greatest commandment, He answered, "Thou shalt love the Lord thy God with all thy heart...and thy neighbour as thyself." Parents can begin to show this by loving their children above all others, and even themselves! Teaching, by its very nature requires us to put our whole effort into helping our own children succeed. If our focus is on helping them, rather than ourselves, then we are following God's plan. We will succeed if we think of ourselves as a thin, flexible "kid glove" that we hold up each day so our God can place His hand in us to do His work. The result is that the fruits of the Spirit will become evident and show themselves in the character that develops in parents and also in the children. If father or mother are focussed in other directions, then the children will assume that God, also, is too busy to be bothered with them.

Jesus' final words to His followers, just before He left to return to heaven, were stated outside Bethany. He said we all were to "preach", "teach", and "make disciples". We have tended to blur these all into one idea, and then to give it to someone else to fulfill. That was not what we were told to do. We have delegated the "teach" to public schools, and the "preach" to pastors. The "make disciples" is, in most cases, left to happen on its own. However, Jesus used these three to show that there are three levels of knowing. We are to be involved in all three! Our children will flourish when we determine to follow Jesus' commands.

In the church we have tended to leave the "preaching" to the pastor on Sundays. Hopefully, our children are being taught in small groups in a Sunday School class. During the week, we have left the "teaching" to the community school teachers. We are hoping that "discipling" will just happen. I strongly believe that many of the negative things that have happened in the last fifty years have something to do with our wrong choices. However, I also believe that we have been given a way to correct our mistakes.

We can take back our given commission and function the way God asked us to. If we do this, we can expect our families to become stronger and our churches to become thriving communities.

Let me describe for you what I call a

Personal,
      Pleasant.
            Prescribed,
                  Purpose,
                        .....with a Promise!

PERSONAL

Jesus walked out of his tomb: the only one Who has ever let Himself out! Forty days later, He met with His disciples for the last time on earth, near Bethany. There, He gave them -- AND Us-- a commission! Each of us, at that time, received a PERSONAL command. We were told to go...and preach...and teach...and make disciples! This was not a command to take people to church so they could listen to a sermon. From God's first instructions, we have been told to begin this process with our own families! From God's revelation through Moses we were all told to teach Who God is, and what He desires, to our own children. It is to be done continually; when they arise, when they are walking, when they are eating, when they are going to bed. (Read Deut. 6) Most of us are guilty of handing this task off to others and we can find many reasons for doing that. However, this wonderful opportunity was actually given to us as parents. We need to take some of it back!

PLEASANT

This opportunity, if understood, is not a difficult, troublesome task that is designed to hold us down or control us. It was given to us to be an incredible blessing to our children and to us parents. While our first thought might be that it would entrap or otherwise hold us back, the reality is that it can be the most liberating of all our activities. Teaching can be PLEASANT for all! It ensures our children understand the family patterns and are given opportunities to grow the way God planned it for them. Teaching them allows our children to understand what is important to us. They feel secure in knowing how to fit in, and become who God made them to be. When children feel secure in their family, they are able to thrive.

PURPOSE

The parents are able to appreciate the children God has given, in a much deeper way when they become involved in teaching. Teaching requires a knowledge of each student. A public school teacher, even when well trained, can't possibly know each child as well as the parent. Children have a built in desire to please the one who is their leader. Mother and Dad have that best opportunity to bond with their own child and provide the best for him or her. As a result, it becomes clear that there is real PURPOSE in this opportunity.

Two questions that need answers, are; "What am I supposed to teach?" and, "How am I supposed to do it?" Most of what follows, deals with both of these. However, I need to pause and explain what many of you may have been already concerned about. You may be already asking, "Is he advocating home schooling and home churching?"

The short answer is "NO!"

I have been involved as a student and educator at all levels of learning from kindergarten to post-graduate university. I have also been involved in helping in several roles in a number of Christian schools, and home-school groups. I think that all of these institutions are managed by dedicated and knowledgeable individuals who are doing many wonderful things to advance the education of our children. All of them deserve to be praised for what they do.

We do need, however, to be aware that they often deal with large groups, and therefore are not quite as able to meet the specific needs of all individuals. The same caution applies to the church. I have been involved for many years in church as worshipper, teacher, and deacon. The Lord blesses greatly when, and if, God is in charge. I do think, however, that many people are sometimes expecting too much of "the church" or "the school" and are not willing to shoulder enough of the load. Both the church and the school should be seen as assistants to the parent. They should never be seen as "The solution!" to your children's education.

Here is the GOOD NEWS! What God is requiring of us has great PURPOSE! He is all about relationship! It was the reason for our creation in the first place. He wants us to love Him and we will understand this best as parents when we build solid relationships with our own children! Here is an opportunity to grasp. I am advocating that we parents take a more intentional approach to the education of our families! You may remember, that this was God's original intention for us. We have arrived in the centre of a system that is trying to do what is best, but we have the opportunity to take it much further. I am not suggesting we should discard what is currently in place, but enhance its effectiveness whenever we can. In the home we actually have the best opportunity to give our children a great start. We already have all the resources needed, and it may actually reduce expenses for "extra curricular programs."

What I am advocating will provide your family with a relationship strengthening process, your children with enhanced learning, and the church with stronger members. Through teaching our own children, we build relationships with them. Through this we begin to understand that the God of the Universe wants us to put Him first and come to Him for all our needs! We will be excited when our children listen to us because we will know that they are wanting to learn. We will be further excited when we see them doing the things that we know will be best for them! God watches for the same things in us! If we teach our children to look outside of themselves to meet the needs of others, we will also begin to understand what God is asking of us.

There is more GOOD NEWS! God has told us what we are to teach, when we are to teach, and how to teach. The curriculum is PRESCRIBED!

Before we look at it, though, let me assure you of one more wonderful thing. It all comes with a PROMISE of success! When Jesus delivered His assignment He ended by saying, "I am with you always, even unto the end…" (Read Matthew 28:19,20). Since He is with us, we can be assured of success if we are doing what He said.

Chapter Two

The children of Israel lived in Egypt for over 400 years. God then called Moses to lead them out, to a land He had promised to Abraham for his descendants. Before they left, God told them to partake in an event they were to celebrate every year from then on. (Exodus 12: 41,42) The Passover was to be remembered as a very significant event in which God had provided supernaturally for their journey.

God not only brought them out of Egypt, but He released them from a life of slavery. He enabled them to all (possibly 3 million) leave the same night, with all of their belongings, and with much of the wealth of Egypt (Exodus 12:35-36). God took them into the desert and supplied all their needs. He personally led them and protected them from the glaring desert sun with a cloud during the day, and He warmed them from the frigid cold of the desert night with fire (Exodus 13:21). He opened a dry path for them through the sea and then closed it to destroy their pursuing enemy (Exodus 14: 29,30). God allowed them to see each of the events that occurred so they would remember (Exodus 14: 31). Each of the amazing events was to help the Israelites remember the ability of their God. They were purposely set out to be teachable lessons so that God's people would be able to introduce the rest of the world to their incredible God. The whole world that God loved was to receive His blessing through this. Unfortunately, it only took them three days to lose sight of the reality of God's ability and begin to complain (Exodus

15: 22-24). God did not abandon them but used every opportunity to teach them as they travelled.

It is from this that we can also learn. We have also departed from the path God has clearly laid out for us. However, He has not left us to develop our own plans. If we call upon Him, He has promised to direct us. We can still pick up the broken pieces of our lives and begin the journey He knows will bless us. We need to understand that, as often as we leave the pathway God has for us, we will lose. We always have the option to return to God, but we will never be able to fully repair the damage we have done while we were trying to do what was in our own hearts. Remember the story of Abraham? He tried to help God out using his own thought and energy. The result was a son of natural birth. God's plan was for him to wait until the birth of the promised son who could only come from God's intervention. Abraham was one hundred years old and Sarah was ninety. Isaac was the son through whom God was to bless the world. Notice that God called Isaac Abraham's only son (Genesis 22: 2). The damage done by Abraham's own effort in an attempt to help God out, has plagued the Israelites ever since. I believe we also have missed out on teaching our children as God instructed us.

God led His people to Mount Sinai where He delivered, through Moses, His Law. It was summarized at the beginning with 10 specific Commandments which set the principles for everything that followed. Later, Jesus further summarized these 10 into one sentence. The first 4 Commandments were summarized into, "Thou shalt love the Lord thy God with all thy heart, with all thy soul, and with all thy strength...." The other 6 were stated as, "...and thy neighbour as thyself." God gave details as to how they were to show their love to God and how to worship Him. Then He set out details about how to love one's neighbour. He also explained how to prevent the spread of disease through good hygiene, and how to be successful as families and as a nation. Following this He cautioned them to do what was expected of them or else bear the consequences of their disobedience. While God had set His love upon these people, He had to punish them for their disobedience many times in the next four thousand years.

From all of this, there are clear patterns for us to follow as fathers and mothers. We have a set of directions for our families and we must make them clear to everyone in the family. Second, we must explain the rewards of following the right pathway and the punishment for disobedience. Finally, we must not miss the chance to reinforce the message in either direction. It must be done thoughtfully and equitably with love. There must be no surprises. Our children have to know the truth!

As part of His Law, God commissioned the parents to teach their children everything they had learned from God. God made it clear that the reason they were to celebrate the Feast of Passover was for the teaching of the children (Exodus 12: 26, 27). Repeatedly, God said that His Works and His Word were to be like frontlets between the eyes, (so they could see the future clearly) on the hand, (so they would work meaningfully) and in the mouth (so they could praise and teach). Later, God had the people make blue fringes to sew on the boarders of their garments so they would have a visual reminder of the results of sin.

In Deuteronomy Chapter 6 God clearly tells the people that He expects them to teach their families. He states the summary that Jesus used (v5) and then commands that they be "in thine heart" (v 6), and that they be taught diligently, to thy children (v7). Note the word "taught" in Hebrew is the same word used to "keenly sharpen" or "whet" a blade. This word does not imply the simple "telling" somebody something. As "sharpening" implies that the end result is a sharpened blade, so this word implies that the child has learned something. The onus here is on the teacher (parent) to ensure the child has grasped the message.

Then (v7) goes on to say that the message should be discussed at any time (perhaps at all times) when sitting in the house and when lying down, and when arising after sleep and when walking outdoors. It is possibly the most important activity for parents. Nowhere else has God commanded us so directly. He said He loves us and because of His love for us He sent Jesus to purchase eternal life. He said, "Teach them!"

The Israelites were rescued out of slavery, led miraculously through the desert, and given God's Law. Each family was then to use God's memory system and teach them for all generations. God taught Moses, Moses taught Joshua, but after Joshua died no one had been taught to carry on. The people began to do "what was right in their own eyes". (see Judges 2: 9-11) Whenever a Judge, a Prophet or a King would focus on what God desired, the people would be brought back into prosperity, and then they would fall away again doing their own thing because the next generation had not been taught. In our world there has been a subtle change away from God that is gathering momentum.

If our children are to know and fear God they must be taught while they are young. An early understanding will enable them to grasp the truths that they will need as they approach the teen years. Trying to reach the teenager who has missed this training is much more difficult for a number of reasons. I believe it is essential to give our primary school children a formal curriculum centered in the home that lifts up their hearts toward God. It is not a difficult task, but like all things of value, it requires commitment.

God made each of our children unique. No one knows them better than the parents. A number of years ago Gary Chapman showed in his book, "The 5 Love Languages" that there are 5 different ways that individuals communicate love. He said that our communication requires us to know the unique "language" of those we are trying to communicate with. Multiply that with the understanding that there are 4 different ways that people learn, and you can begin to see why education was given to the parents.

God knows that you have the best opportunity to reach your children. No human can love a child more than the parents, and no human cares more to see them succeed in life. No one, except God, knows the mind of the child better than the parents. Even a well-trained teacher cannot teach over 20 students at one time, who are all individually different, as well as the parents who know each of their children's nature best!

Chapter Three

After 60 years as a part of the church of Jesus Christ, having talked with saints, listened to many sermons, and observed results, I have come to the realization that the church of the "western" nations could be and should be re-examining Christ's great commission. It is clear from Matt. 28 that ALL the people who make up the church are to preach, teach, and make disciples. The Christians of the western church have focused on the preaching of the Word almost exclusively. We have been instructed to preach the Gospel, and this has been fulfilled fairly well. However, instead of teaching Christ's commands, we have used the same preaching strategy to tell people how they should live; but <u>preaching</u> is not <u>teaching</u>. As far as "discipling" is concerned, very little has been done!

More than 50 years as an educator has given me insights into how the commission could be fulfilled, but let me begin with an overview. It deals with the spiritual condition of youth and the faulty expectations we parents have had of thinking that the church could meet all their needs, without much input from us!

Young people who have grown up around the church have often made starts toward following God and have then left what they believe is an irrelevant community. They have looked at the world around them and they have not seen that "faith in God" is of any practical use. The God they know, will not help them get better marks in school, not help them find a job, not help them play sports, and definitely not help them make friends or fit in with the rest of the school.

'Fitting-in', to them, is absolutely essential. They sometimes demonstrate an interest in knowing what God wants them to do in specific situations. Whether this is an interest in really knowing God's will or not could be debated. Probably in some cases it is indeed so. In many cases, it is a matter of finding out and then deciding whether the specific decision should be made in God's will or whether they would feel better served by going according to the paths of their peers. The result is often unsatisfactory, and they either leave the church community or, if required by family, attend church sessions with both ears and brain tuned out.

They reason that this is necessary so they can whole-heartedly fit in with what they perceive as the "real" world. If they continue "in church" they often assume that the problem they sense is with "their church" and that moving to a new congregation will give them what they are looking for. Without teaching, they begin a life of church hopping, at best, or leave altogether. They often do not learn that "the church" is a community of believers who believe what God has said. They think, instead, it is a place – a building - where people "go" to hear about an ancient lifestyle, and be entertained.

To many people, in the outside world, a church is seen as a sort of museum where one should be able to see, on display, representatives of holiness! In reality, a better concept is that a church is more like a hospital, where those who know they need God's help, have come to get well! None of us can claim to have reached God's goal for us – to become like His Son!

We, who are the church, can choose to blame the youth in order to ease our conscience, or we can choose to face up to the reality that we have not given them the teaching they needed. Many of them are lost to worldliness or even lost to systems of men that counterfeit the truth, thinking that they are following God's precepts. Let's choose to begin now to rectify our path and follow the Lord.

There are three things we can do to bring about the changes necessary. The first is to understand that the needed teaching should not be the sole responsibility of the local church. For too long we have expected that a 40 minute Sunday School "lesson" is all that is needed for our children to learn the truths of God. This is a fallacy. Sixty years ago, when the most of society tended to reinforce the Sunday School lesson, it may have been enough, but not now. Teaching takes time; a lot more time than 40 minutes a week. Our children are hearing and seeing 80 hours a week of counter arguments through school and various media. Secondly, we need to shoulder some of the responsibility to do the teaching at home in the most natural setting. Thirdly, we need to learn what teaching entails and how to do it. It is not difficult, but it does require time and preparation. The eternal benefits are well worth any amount of time spent on this endeavour.

I would like you, now, to examine, your commission. It was one of the last things Jesus Christ stated before He went to heaven. It consists of three parts (preach, teach, make disciples), but we need to read its statement from the two men who recorded it from the words of the Master. (Notice particularly, the original words and their meanings.)

THE GREAT COMMISSION

Mark 16:15
Go ye into all the world, and preach (kerusso)* the gospel to every creature.

> (kerusso means to proclaim or tell)

Matthew 28:19

Go... and teach (matheteuo)* all nations...

    (matheteuo means to make disciples of)

Matthew 28:20

...teaching them (didasko)* to observe all things whatsoever I have commanded you

    (didasko means to impart instruction)

Note that in the original text three different words were used;

    Kerusso, to proclaim or tell,

    Didasko, to impart instruction,

    Matheteuo, to make disciples of.

Jesus followed this by saying,

    "and, lo, I am with you always,

        even unto the end of the age."

Jesus gave us our orders!

    "Go preach,... teach, ...and make disciples."

  He then promised He would be right alongside to coach us to the finish.

  Few of us in the western church may have experienced the teaching and the discipling that is commanded here. We may be used to hearing Sunday School lessons or a Pastor's weekly sermon. We may have made an effort to attend series of sermons on particular facets of the Christian way, but we may not remember having been taught in depth or discipled in our Christian experience. As a result, we may think that this is not something to become involved in. However, the commission presented by the Saviour is something that we were all given to do!

Our children need to be taught in more depth than we were. They are living in a very different world than we grew up in. If you actually did experience a period of teaching, then use what you know to help others. Many may decide to attempt what I am outlining here, but they may need help to put it into practice.

Since Jesus gave us our orders, and since He promised to be with us in their fulfillment, we can be sure it is a do-able task. Our commitment to learning and fulfilling our commission will bring us joy and blessing beyond what words can express.

Let us now have a look at the three levels of knowing implicit in the three words, Preach, Teach, and Make Disciples.

PREACHING

Preaching literally means announcing or proclaiming information. We are told to tell people worldwide about the wonderful news of the Gospel. The church has been best at fulfilling this part of the command. The process of telling, proclaiming, or announcing is required to capture the attention of the passersby to alert them to their condition and point out to them a way of escape. It is often ineffective to awaken the masses to their need and to introduce new information. Its primary purpose is to proclaim that God is Love, and that He has provided all that is needful for us all. An awareness of these issues reaches only the first level of knowing. Unfortunately, preaching has been tried as an easy process to fulfill our second responsibility; that of teaching, but it is ineffective for the task of reaching more than a quarter of the people!

(more on this later)

TEACHING

Teaching is not the same as telling (preaching): it uses a different technique, often in small groups, and has a different purpose and outcome. Jesus told us to "teach them to observe the commands" that He left us. The process of teaching goes much deeper than "telling them about" the commands. We might preach or tell about the 50 or so commands of Christ, and even tell what they are designed to accomplish, but we are told to "teach" them and this is very different.

We have come to regard teaching as anything one does to pass on ideas to others. However, in our modern world of instant coffee and drive through restaurants we have substituted the art of teaching with a quick fix. It is no wonder our children have missed the message. We have told them what to do, what to think, and what to believe. They have no foundation to build on. All around them they are subjected to impressionable images and messages that seem all too good. Their peers buy into the world's values but they have no foundation in truth, like the man who built on sand. I am trying to explain here that true teaching will give our children understanding to do the right thing, understanding to think correctly, and understanding to support strong convictions.

Teaching infers learning and if a would-be pupil does not learn then teaching has not occurred. A preacher can effectively "deliver the sermon" even if the audience does not respond. It is not so with teaching! A teacher is only teaching when the students are given the resources and enabled to actually learn the lesson material, from the inside out. The purpose of teaching is to nurture understanding of what is, and how it relates to all other issues surrounding it. The teacher is there to aid the students who actually do the learning through a carefully prepared series of steps, sometimes uniquely designed for each student. By the time a student has "learned" a concept it has become part of his or her thinking and change has occurred. The student has reached an understanding, which is the goal of this second level of knowing.

Some might say that they can't teach or that they don't know how. I submit that all parents are already involved in teaching lessons to their children, and usually with good success. Where there is a necessity, it happens. We teach children why crossing the road is dangerous and we teach them the importance of reacting properly to traffic lights, and angry dogs. Children learn that they will not be given freedom to cross the road until they have demonstrated clearly that they have learned the skills necessary. In most homes children learn early on that they will not be served the dessert until they have cleaned up the first course at dinner. (more of this later)

MAKING DISCIPLES

The third part of the great commission tells us to make disciples of all nations. It comes about in a one-on-one relationship between a disciple and a "disciple-in-training". This is a slow and methodical process where the understandings of the "disciple-in-training" are tested in real-world situations and the experiences are evaluated against scripture. The process may take months or years and continue until the disciple convinces the new disciple that he or she is ready and committed to actually apply the learning to real world situations.

The second phase of learning to be a disciple begins when the "disciple in training' takes on a new believer and begins to disciple this one in the same way they were discipled.

This third level of knowing, is the stage in which the "ought-to-bes" become the normal pattern of life. A young child is soon aware that walking would be an asset. With much effort he stumbles and falls but soon is able to stand and even walk with some difficulty. With help from others and a great deal of self-determination and coaching (discipling) the concept is internalized and eventually walking is second nature and goes on without much further thought. He has reached the third level of knowing (about walking) .

The three levels of knowing, have been expressed in many ways; - awareness, understanding, and function; or recognition, structure, and replication; or knowing what a passage of scripture says, knowing what the passage means, and ensuring it operates for me in my world. These three levels of learning can themselves be understood and learned by those who wish the skills. In fact, to some extent most of us use them regularly with our own children or with employees. Let's examine them in a little more detail.

PREACHNG	results in	AWARENESS
TEACHING	results in	UNDERSTANDING
DISCIPLING	results in	APPLICATION

LEVEL ONE – AWARENESS

This is a beginning stage where the individual becomes aware of, and somewhat conversant with an issue. It is where a child begins all knowing, and where an adult is confronted with new information. Two weeks ago I told my 2 year old granddaughter that the shiny silver thing moving across the blue sky was an airplane. Yesterday, while watching her sister play soccer she pointed to the sky and said, "Airplane!" Does she know about airplanes? No, she is only aware that the silver thing moving across the blue sky is called an airplane because that is what she was told. Now if I try to tell her that all airplanes are not silver, do not sound the same, actually land on the ground, or transport persons, a different process will be necessary. Merely "telling" her these things will have no meaning.

In the spiritual realm, the Lord has made it possible for the simplest of us to grasp, through telling and hearing, the most important truths of all. Children, at a very young age, can grasp an awareness of sin, God's love and provision, and their need to respond. God doesn't require them, or any of us, to fully understand the awfulness of sin, or the depths to which Jesus came to lift us out of the mirey clay and set our feet upon a rock, before we can become His children. Once we are aware of a truth, however, we must be taught deeper insights, or the blessings that could be ours will be stifled. It would be like reading a passage of the scriptures, and then moving on the next and the next without understanding what has already been read! Or perhaps, it would be like listening to sermon after sermon without really taking the time to understand the deeper implications about what has been told.

LEVEL TWO – UNDERSTANDING

This is a much more involved stage where an individual moves past the awareness of an issue or idea to the understanding of it. The process by which this development occurs is fueled by the desire of the student, and not the teacher. The desire of the student is harnessed in one of 4 ways. One quarter of any population fits into each of these ways. (see Chapter 6) A teacher, when attempting to stimulate learning, needs to provide the appropriate environment for each type of student. The ancient notion that every head is an empty vessel into which knowledge is poured has been proven false.

Learning is done by the student, who is encouraged by the teacher (parent). The teacher encourages through questioning, and setting up the appropriate environment. The teacher knows when teaching has been done because of the response. The word used by the Master was "Didasko", to impart instruction. The teacher has imparted knowledge when the student responds with positive excitement to the new knowledge. In this, the teacher needs to ascertain the difference between the student relating what he or she feels the teacher wants to hear, and what the student truly believes.

In this environment, the student discovers new knowledge, and as more and more knowledge is attained, the interaction of one part connects with other parts until the student exclaims, "Eureka, I see how it all fits!" Understanding has been recognized by the student. Something has changed within, and attitudes and commitments will follow.

Commitments develop as convictions are established within the learner that, for example, scriptures are objective truth – the inerrant Word of the living God. It is through the convictions that the learner becomes a disciple 'in training' and to this level of knowing that the great commission points us.

If I want my little granddaughter who was referred to above, to understand a larger concept of "airplane" I can't tell her more than she can grasp. I could take her to an airport and let her watch people walk out to a 'thing' on the ground that she may call a car, or weird bus. If she continues to watch it taxi to the runway and eventually take off and become a silvery 'thing' in the blue sky, she will have "discovered" for herself some more knowledge and she might even call those 'things' on the ground, "Airplanes!" As she gains maturity she may actually take an interest in flying, but there would be a great deal of learning required before she would be able to actually fly an aircraft. In this case, more than teaching would be necessary. Even with extensive learning about aircraft and the rules of flying, she would not be able to take me flying. Another level of knowing would be required consisting of another process called discipling (or coaching).

LEVEL THREE - TRANSFER OR APPLICATION

The third level of knowing requires a third process. The Bible calls it discipling, and Jesus left it as the ultimate commission, "Make disciples of all nations." In this process, the student receives private tutoring because the outcome is not to make the recipient like everyone else, but to encourage the development of this unique individual to reach the full potential of God's design. The tutor basically walks along beside the student who is becoming the disciple, and together they examine God's principles as they apply to the moment by moment experiences of life. Notice that the Tutor (or coach) does not do the learning for his learner, any more than a running coach can exercise on behalf of his learner.

What did Jesus do when He wanted His disciples to know His ability to rule nature? Did He sit them down and <u>tell</u> them what He knew and about all His power? No! He accompanied those fishermen out on a boat into their known element and then He set up a scenario that would catch their attention in a new way. Those fishermen became emotional about their situation and their experience resulted in new knowledge. They found out that this friend of theirs could control the elements! Sometime later He sent them back again and offered to help them in their new struggle. He walked on the water as if He would go past. The disciples (in training) learned this time that they could call on Him to help them personally whenever they needed Him. Discipleship training is not a curriculum based activity with a specific goal that everyone should reach, and even after the tutor has stepped aside the new disciple continues the process of learning. In fact, the process intensifies for the new disciple who now becomes a tutor to a new student.

It is probable that the new disciple actually grows faster, as the role of tutor requires even more learning. Paul's second letter to Timothy outlines the process (chapter 2, verse 2) – "The things which you have heard from me (during our walk in the big world), these entrust to faithful men, who will be able to teach others also."

In the homey version of my granddaughter's learning to take me flying, she would be required to go through every conceivable action that relates to applying all her understanding of flight in a specific aircraft with a trained pilot on the seat beside her. The trained pilot, the disciple of flying, knows what is required and as they spend many hours together she is gradually trained (discipled) to become a qualified pilot. When the instructor is convinced she can fly, and is also able to convince her that she is able to fly, she is left to do a solo circuit. If that is successful, she is then required to practice maneuvers to perfection. If she wants to learn it best, she should then learn to train another pilot. That is the secret of success in 2 Tim. 2:2.

EVERYONE IS COMMISSIONED TO

DISCIPLE OTHERS (ALSO)

------- EVEN YOU!! -----

❧ PART TWO ❧

I have discussed why we should engage in teaching our own children. In what follows, I will assume that most readers will be attempting, at some level, to engage their children in the home environment. You need to decide if it will be as enrichment added to what is already being learned in the local public school, church, or your home-schooling programme. If you choose to take on the entire task, you will find many resources for home-schooling already available for teaching the public school components of Language, Mathematics, Social Studies, Science, etc. I will refer to these, but focus on the parts that have been left out regarding God's curriculum.

In beginning this section, we need to consider the difference between what happens in a local public school, and what you will be able to do in your home. In a public school, a teacher is given a prescribed curriculum, in which all the courses are laid out. The curriculum, there, is about facts and ideas. (Most teachers also know that something else is more important than those facts. A complete education is more about quality of life and character development, but it is only "hoped" that these will develop, as they are not measured or fully assessed.)

Before we actually begin, however, it is very important for you to get possession of three keys! Without these keys, little of significance will result!

KEY ONE

Please note that God's promises are for <u>His people</u>. In order to benefit from them, you must be, or become, a member of His family.

Jesus said He was the only way to God. He loves you! He died for you! He has paid for everything you have ever done wrong, or ever will do! He holds out to you a free pardon, and an invitation to become part of His forever family! It is free for you, because He has already paid the price! In John 3, Jesus said, "You must be born again!"

KEY TWO

Endeavour to get to really <u>know</u> God! When you begin to "delight in Him", He <u>gives you</u> the desires of <u>your</u> heart (Psalm 37:4)

KEY THREE

Learn all you can and do your best -BUT- <u>never</u> rely on your own strength or ability! It is God who promises your success <u>when</u> you put your trust in <u>HIM</u>.

With these three keys in your possession, we can begin this section. Consider the difference between what happens in a local public school and what you will be able to do in your home. In a public school, a teacher is given a prescribed curriculum, in which all the courses are laid out. The curriculum, there, is mostly about facts and ideas. (Most teachers also know that something else is more important than those facts. A complete education is more about quality of life and character development, but it is only "hoped" that these will develop, as they are not measured or fully assessed.)

The principles of teaching are also set forth, and each curriculum component is given a time slot, in which assignments are completed. A trained teacher is required to move at a prescribed pace and bring as many pupils as possible to its successful conclusion. The teacher does the best that can be done under those restrictions.

The home situation is very different, and allows the parents to establish the home curriculum, and to set schedules for learning that are compatible with their own children and other family commitments. The local authorities can assess that each child is receiving learning of the publicly prescribed part of the curriculum. Carefully, thought out, home schooling can be very successful, and provide a good start toward University studies.

For the rest of this document I will use the term teacher to refer to Mom and Dad who are taking up, at least part of, this task with their family. I will still use it, of course, when referring to those who have made a career of teaching as a vocation.

"What to teach," "When to teach," and "How to teach" are dramatically different in the home than they are in the public classroom. In the Christian home these three are closely and vitally connected. We are not just to "teach", but are to "make disciples".

Further, it has been shown that you can be your child's best teacher since you know your child better than anyone else. However, please be aware that this works in two ways! Not only do you know your child best, but also your child knows you best! Connect that to the known fact that the child learns best what they see being done, rather than by what they are told. As a result of these, there is a great deal of pressure on the parent to <u>demonstrate clearly</u>, what it is they wish the child to emulate.

God has built in this "boomerang" effect. In the same way, as the parent follows God's direction and demonstrates acceptance and obedience of the truth, the children will learn to accept God's Word and obey His commands. It works like this. Our love for God teaches us to know and obey God so that our children, whom we also love, will do as we are doing. There is great incentive coming from both directions. We have two reasons to study God's Word daily for direction. This should encourage parents to develop an authentic life-style without compromises. Therefore, you may need to ask God to help you remove disharmony and any dysfunction from your home. Great teaching will then result in discipleship training, leading to God's best for your children, who could go onward to form families of disciples also.

You probably already know that children are very perceptive. They can sense anything that is not authentic. They watch what you read, and watch what interests you on TV. They will never accept ideas that sound like, "I know this little thing is not what God would wish, but when you get older you will understand why adults do things like this." The children know how much you believe God by how you operate. The evil one, also, will make sure that your children get the subtle negative messages because he wants them to miss out on the blessings that God wants to give them.

Let's face it. The alternatives are horrendous! Jesus spent a lot more time describing hell than heaven. He tried to warn us of the nature of that place that was designed for the devil and his angels. It was described as a place of loneliness where the only thing a person will be left with will be memories of what could have been! Let's teach God's love as demonstrated by Jesus when He left His home above, and entered our world through a young woman in a small town called Bethlehem just so He could grow up and die for each of us! He is the ultimate hero that almost all stories try to hook on to. None of them are even close to the real one.

God wants each of us, including your children, to accept adoption papers that are already paid for, so we can sit with Jesus at His Father's table! Most of the people, who are part of that family, accepted the offer before they were old enough to enter High School. Our task is to help our children understand the realities while they are young.

Once they accept God's offer and accept Him as Saviour, our task of helping them become disciples begins in earnest. It flows alongside the teaching, because now there is a new application of the truth, which changes a person's perception and actions. There is a new reason for living. A love for God will change a person's focus. They can take on the exciting role of serving their God for the benefit of others.

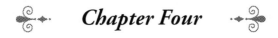

Chapter Four

WHAT SHOULD I TEACH?

THE CURRICULUM

I n the public school, each teacher is given the curriculum, which is produced in a province or state by a team of professionals. It describes what the teacher is to teach to the students in the class. It focuses on a number of things it is deemed worth knowing. In mathematics we study how to use numbers. Art focuses on a way to find expression through drawing and painting. In science, the nature of the physical and biological world is investigated. However, most educators know that the real purpose of learning is about meeting deeper needs. "Educated persons" are supposed to be able to care for themselves. They should be able to fit into their local society, be able to work at employment and contribute to the benefits of those less able. That means the curriculum should help develop good character. Each person should be truthful, trustworthy and productive.

God's curriculum aims at all of these by giving it in the Law through Moses, by reinforcing it through Jesus, and by all the writers of the Bible. These important issues are very difficult to evaluate. As a result, only the mathematics, art, science, etc., are graded. Parents need to know that God's Word is much more able to provide leadership in the more important areas that define character. Once a child learns what Jesus has done for them personally, and commits his or her life to the Saviour, the Spirit, in turn, will begin to aid the child to develop the Fruits of the Spirit, which appear as good character. Therefore, in the home, it is the Bible and its presentation of God that should become the curriculum.

The Great Commission gave us three levels of knowing. The scriptures will provide the awesome reality of God and His attributes. The children, under your direction, will find HIM to be truthful, loving, powerful, and One to go to for every need! We need to share our own story of finding, and receiving God. If our stories and our attitudes are positive, the children will want to believe in the God Who has done so much for them. Once they do, we need to teach them how to share their story with friends. Nothing in life is more exciting than leading another to your Saviour! If it becomes deeply rooted in them and clearly understood, they will become disciples with convictions about their faith. As a result they will develop relationships with others of like mind in the church. Their convictions will drive them, through the love of Christ, to "love their neighbours as themselves!" Their families will also follow Christ!

Old Testament Stories can be great starting places for many lessons. They show how God took a family of nomadic shepherds and made them the greatest kingdom on earth under David and Solomon. God previously took the youngest son in a large family of shepherds, who was treated terribly by his family, and sold as a slave. This slave then became a prison convict for following God! After several years in prison, he was taken out and in one day he was made the second in command of the largest nation on earth! In spite of God's many, many manifestations of His power and care, Gods "family" chose often to act opposite to His direction! Over and over, God lamented that His people chose to reject Him! They even chose to worship gods made by their own hands! They even chose to sacrifice their own babies in fires to their pretend gods!

We can learn from all of this that:

1. Our families will not always follow what is best.
2. God knows what it is to experience failures.
3. God knows our pain as we watch our family struggle.
4. We need to love those who step out of line.
5. If they return to Him they can be forgiven.
6. <u>Like the parent in Luke 15, we watch for their return.</u>

As indicated above, good teaching does not always bear good fruit when we expect it! In the story Jesus told of the prodigal son, there was a father, who reminds us of God – our Father. This father did all he could, but then, he watched, and waited. He probably prayed! The best any of us can do is to keep ourselves connected to Jesus and live with His resources flowing through us to our children. Teaching, done for the right reason, will benefit the student more than the teacher. It becomes a gift from our Master, and we become His conduit!

The ultimate goal in teaching is never to direct our children down a pathway we choose for them. Rather, it is for us to be so tightly grafted into Jesus (our vine) that His life flows through us to directly nurture them. God already has a pathway chosen for each of our students. We are to help them find it and then, with constant prayer, watch them choose His guidance.

God will never force any of us to obey Him. Loving obedience must be given willfully. It is the only evidence that we or our children are actually part of God's forever family. It is from this that anyone is actually able to…"love the LORD your GOD with all your heart… and your neighbour as yourself."

The father, in Jesus' story, never gave up praying for, and

watching for his son's return. Nor did he blame himself, but believed that God was in control. In that time period, any neighbour who saw that "unruly son" could have killed him. The father was so intent on forgiveness, that he was the first to see him coming home! His quick action demonstrated his unconditional love for his child.

TEACH LEARNING SKILLS

Our children need to be given the tools to continue their own learning when the formal lessons have ended. As a result, we need to build in opportunities for them to understand the value of learning, and of making decisions. These long-term goals need to be given room to mature throughout their learning years. It will happen if we build opportunities into their experiences.

For example, the value of learning can be approached by giving an assignment with a reward for the process that was used. Don't always give a reward for a well finished thing. You should try to praise whatever is done in an excellent fashion. (Be sure to highlight the character qualities above the items done. The ultimate goal is to develop good character.) To do this you could assign a project related to an interest of your child. If the idea of oil painting is drawing them, then assign a study of the art form. Perhaps you could offer that if the study is reported on well because "they did their best", a set of oils and an easel will be awarded.

TEACH DECISION MAKING

Similarly, the child needs to develop the understanding that making good decisions is very important. It is easiest for parents to make decisions that we think will be best for our children. However, we need to teach them how to find good advice outside the home, and how to become confident in the advice of experts in many fields. They will only be weaned off the parent by practicing this important skill. This is also important for if they cannot look past the home for advice, they will not be able to even trust God!

TEACH THE BIBLICAL PATTERN OF HANDLING MONEY

It may seem that this is not a topic on the level of the last two, but more stress in our society is developed from a lack here than for most other issues. God's pattern has been shown to far exceed any other in this regard. Many books have been written on this subject and the effective ones all follow God's plan!

THE GIVEN CURRICULUM (GOD'S PLAN)

At the giving of the Law, we were told to teach what God had given through Moses. Children were to memorize the commandments and understand them. They were to embed them in their brains, (to control their thinking) attach them to their arms (to help control their actions) and they were to be attached to the doors of their houses, (to control family activities and relationships). Jesus restated them again when He described, in one breath, the focus of them all, "You shall love the Lord your God with all of your being, (body, soul, spirit) and your neighbour as yourself"

TEACH THE 10 COMMANDMENTS

To focus on the relevance of each of the 10 commandments would be a great starting point. Yes, it would be good to help them memorize all ten, but the teaching goes well past just learning the words! Children should begin to understand what each means and why it is important. For example, a family is the best place to grasp what it means to honour your Father and Mother! This commandment comes with a promise – a promise for a longer life! We are able to teach this important command by demonstrating it in the way we, in turn, honour the parents that gave themselves to us for a major part of their lives. If we, as parents, put our aging parents, ahead of our personal wants, we will be cared for by our children when they are older. The greatest benefit is that your children will understand what it means to put God first in their lives. This is, after all, a first step to understanding what God expects of each of us It also gives us a practical view of our inability to live the commandments out in our own strength. As the New Testament points out, they were not given for us to keep, but to show us that we are unable to meet God's standard on our own. It is why Jesus had to come and pay our debt, so we could become part of His forever family.

This whole study could be expanded as children grow older, by studying the rest of what God said in terms of Feast celebrations, the various offerings and how each points to an aspect of what Jesus did for us. Every aspect of the physical tabernacle and its functioning gives us a picture of our Saviour! There is enough in this to provide themes for several years or parts of them.

TEACH THE COMMANDS OF CHRIST

Another source of curriculum comes directly from the Great Commission. We were told that our job is to "Teach the commands" that Jesus gave us. There are approximately 50 specific commands that we were told to keep. If we studied one of these as a theme each week it would take a year to go over them once. Just working with His commands could provide a spiral curriculum, that could be revisited periodically, gradually going deeper into them as the children grow older. For example: One of those commands is, "Follow me!" (Matt. 4:19) The curriculum could focus on this one command for many sessions. One could ask, "What does it mean to follow Jesus?" "What would we need to know in order to follow Jesus?" "What would we gain by following Jesus?" "What might happen if we don't?"etc. Rather than just discuss this issue, you could set up a "game" by having someone go out ahead into a forest, and ask the others what we need to know to be able to follow? Would it be helpful to know something about the ways of the person who was chosen? Could we trust the one we were to follow? If we can't actually see the person who is somewhere in the forest, how can we follow? Will there be some reward if we are able to follow? If we can see the person, would it be easier?

Personally, I think the most important goal in teaching children should be to intentionally lead them to salvation. Most decisions to follow Jesus Christ as Lord, occur before a child leaves elementary school age! Nothing is more important. It is critical to point out that this does not involve a "say after me these words" mantra. A child needs to KNOW the fact of their naturally sinful nature! They need to KNOW that Jesus is God!

They need to KNOW that Jesus actually died for them on a Roman cross outside of Jerusalem. They must learn that they can only be part of God's forever family, by personally thanking Jesus for paying their sin debt. They must learn that they must personally pray to Jesus and ask Him to come and live within and take over as their Lord! (Romans 10:9).

It is important to carefully consider their level of commitment. It is not enough for them to state, "Yes I believe." I have been told that in areas in Korea, a new believer will not be baptized until they have shown that they are a believer by bringing someone to salvation! My own father used to say that if the 12 disciples, in their lifetime, had only brought one each to Jesus, and if those had done the same through time, there would still only be 12!

Dad's solution was that each should endeavour to bring at least 2, so there could be a multiplication factor. Then, with a twinkle in his eye he always followed by saying that once you have had the thrill of bringing two, you will never stop looking for others!

Someone may say that we should not 'bother' others with our religion. If we really believe that Jesus is the only way, and that without Him everyone is lost, then we need to respond whether we feel like it or not! If you were walking down your street and saw your neighbour's house on fire, would you not rush to the window or door and awaken them to save their physical lives? The soul is far more precious and eternity is a very longtime!

Once your children have committed themselves to God, have them memorize passages of scripture and work to develop, within them, a longing for intimacy with God! There are many writers who have prepared ways of doing this. Just understanding Who our great God is would lead the way. Three books come immediately to mind, in this regard.

Robert J. Morgan wrote a helpful book: "100 Bible Verses everyone should know by heart"

Phillip Keller wrote "What is the Father Like?"

He used 17 short chapters to examine the "I AM"s . I AM; the Author, the Word, Almighty, Truth, Mercy, Understanding, Grace, Long-Suffering, the Saviour, Joy, Faithful, Good, Love, Peace, Moderation, the Way, Righteous and Just, Holy!

A wonderful list was produced by Neil T. Anderson and has appeared in more than one of his books. They appear in "Rough Road to Freedom", and they list "The Believer's Identity In Christ"p124.

I am accepted:	John 1:12	I am God's child
	John 15:15	I am Jesus' chosen friend….
I am secure:	Romans 8:1-2	I am free from condemnation
	Romans 8:28	I am assured that all things work together for good…
I am significant	Matthew 5: 13-16	I am the salt and light for everyone around me
	John 15: 1,5	I am a part of the true vine, joined to Christ and able to produce much fruit….

Etc………. Etc…….. Etc………

"66 Love Letters", by Dr. Larry Crabb could be a wonderful read for teenagers. It goes through the entire Bible, giving a two to three page overview of each book! Dr. Crabb understands human thought and really does provide soul-searching questions and answers.

These and many other resources are available. Don't feel as if you must develop all your own resources. Let the Lord lead you. He cares about your family and you in ways none of us will ever be able to understand. He loves you! He loves your family! He yearns for you to come to Him and listen and learn what He has for your success! I will include at the end, several books I have found personally helpful. But the possibilities are almost endless.

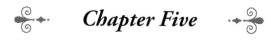

Chapter Five

WHEN SHOULD I TEACH?

THE SCHEDULE

F
or the public classroom, the local school plans the timetable and the rate at which each subject should be encountered. This is somewhat contrived and artificial because every student has different approaches and needs. At home one can decide on a schedule, but one is not "locked into it". This provides another great advantage in learning in the family situation.

Earlier, it was pointed out, that it is critical that you know the learner. Knowing the moment by moment life patterns and events are also important. The home can easily adjust the time needed in each situation for each learner. I observed, on one occasion, a class that was somewhat "interrupted" by blaring fire trucks as they arrived at a house directly opposite to the classroom. They were there to rescue people and put out a fire. The teacher was upset by the "distraction" and closed the blackout drapes so the present lesson could continue. It was, apparently, the "wrong time" of the week for a lesson on community services!

Hopefully, in the home environment, such opportunities will be grasped as they arise in the course of living and not discarded as a nuisance. God is standing by, and because of His interest in our families, He will provide the opportunities that are needed for each of our children at just the right time!

Here is another issue to think about! We live our life in the home. We don't arrive there each day for a "lesson". The fact is, rather, that we are all constantly learning in the home. The real question, then, is not, "When should I teach?" The real question is, "How consistent is my on-going lesson?" If we are all learning at all times, it is important to evaluate the structure of the home environment. A new small book by Robert J. Morgan, "Mastering Life" sets out 10 simple, yet profound things we can do to set our life, and home, in order. Each of these scriptural principles should be part of our teaching. He deals with the organization and use of time, the value of patterns and placing things where they belong. He demonstrates that such order, makes life run more efficiently, with less waste, and it actually reduces costs. It would be another great place to start! It could be revisited as needed.

Children learn to do what is "observed" more easily than by what is told them. They pick up home patterns, and attitudes without even trying to learn them. It is essential, therefore, that parents constantly exhibit the patterns they hope to develop within their children. If one observes some unwanted behaviour in a child, it may be a reflection of what they have seen. We, perhaps, should check a mirror before beginning to criticize what happened. For the benefit of our children, it may be necessary to change our behaviour patterns out of love for our offspring! Children have a built in sense of fairness. It is clearly put there by their Creator.

It would be wise for each of us to examine our own patterns of behavior on a regular basis. We could do this independently, but it would be much better for all concerned if it was done in conjunction with a spouse, since both parents are involved in the teaching. It would result in much better harmony, sort of like an orchestra that had actually practiced together!

A good way to begin such a procedure would involve both parents making a well thought-out listing of those qualities they would hope to see develop in the children. Follow that with some evidences of behavior that would demonstrate their development. That list could be used by the parents to assess the growth in the children on a periodic review of their accomplishments. It could also be used periodically by the parents as a personal assessment of their growth to give them the confidence they may need to carry on, even when times are tough.

It is inappropriate for adults to tell their children that what they observe being done by adults should not be done by them now, but will somehow become legitimate for them when they get older! The spiritual laws don't change with time. I have found that science can help us understand this. The fact is that the physical laws, for example, do not change. The force of gravity gives a good example. Sir Isaac Newton back about 300 years ago studied gravity and came up with an equation that is still in operation to-day. It helped put men on the moon in my lifetime! The force of gravity is something like God, in that it never changes. It is the same throughout the entire Universe. It doesn't matter what one's skin colour is, what one's nationality, sex or age is. It works the same for everyone; for a baby that falls out of a carriage and for an old man who falls off the roof! It also is so unique that science has not been able to figure out how it works!

As a result of this, we can teach best when we focus on Real Issues; that is, on what your children see as real! In other words, take advantage of real life events as they come up. Since we cannot easily cause some of those "real life events", we should watch for them and use them whenever they appear. If we believe that our God loves us and our children and that He has a path for each of us to follow, it is not a stretch of the mind to realize that our God can, and will provide opportunities for us to learn as He sees fit.

It is important for us to use what we know of our children and what God has left for us. In this way we can balance the many parts in order to provide a broad focus. Our Creator had a plan for each of our children and He may decide to bring along a diversion from our plan. It is important for us to be prepared to go the new way. For example, you may be working on the history of your neighbourhood, but one of your children joins a sport club to play soccer or ice hockey. You would have the option to defer the current study so that you are in tune with the new venture. It might be worth looking into the physics of motion, friction, forces, air pressure, or any number of studies that relate to the new team adventure. It would also be a great time to study the advantages of being a team-player, rather than the team "hot-shot".

When should I teach?

The reality is that we are <u>always teaching</u> --- something!

Chapter Six

HOW SHOULD I TEACH

I 'm going to assume that most readers are not trained educators. I have spent my life in the field, but I am not going to begin this section with the latest theories about how children learn. That will come later when, and if, you decide to read it. This part is for "beginners". As I have said earlier, you already have been teaching but may not realize it. I would like you to begin where you are. Here are some thoughts that may help you get started on this new venture toward becoming more intentional in working with your children.

Begin by asking yourself a few questions. What do I enjoy doing? What activities make me happiest? What do each of my children find most interesting, or enjoy doing the most? The answers to these questions could provide the place where you should begin your teaching. You will inspire your children to perform and understand what you want them to learn when they watch your excitement as you do what you love doing! These starting points will lead to more meaningful learning, because out of them will come opportunities to look to the next level of learning. From then on, keep your ear open to listen for the next thing to work with. If your attitude is that you want to please God, just begin to act, and if you ask Him, "He will make your path straight" (Proverbs 3:6)

Let me give you an early experience I had. My life has been focussed on the physical and biological world of God's creation. One evening at the dinner table, my oldest daughter was filling us in on her day at the Christian school. She said she had a science experiment to write up for homework. My ears immediately were focussed and I asked what experiment she had performed. She said her homework was to write out the experiment they had read about that day in their book. I did a double take and asked for clarification. The teacher had read with them, that if they filled a glass with water, and then placed a piece of paper over the glass, leaving out any air bubbles, they could then turn the glass upside down and the paper would hold the water in the glass! I was not sure what she had actually told me, so I asked, "Did it work?" The vibes I had detected were real! They had not actually tried it, but they were to assume it was true and write a note to that effect!!! Here was my big chance! I said, "Try it! Get a glass out of the cupboard, and do what you said the book said to do, then write up what actually happened." She was skeptical, because she knew the teacher wanted her note to have the "right" information. I'm not sure she actually thought it would work. However, she followed the method, and in a few moments she exploded with excitement! "IT WORKED! IT ACTUALLY WORKED!!"

It was a thrill for me to watch her excitement. She learned a great deal, but it was not a planned lesson. Always try to stay alert to those situations. If you, or your children enjoy baking or cooking, then work together on the production of whatever interests them. In doing so, many other messages can be built in. If they love baking, watch how they function and step in as the opportunity comes up. Stay with them as you are able. Help them read every detail, and question them as to what might happen if they missed one of the ingredients, or measured in error? If the result is less than desirable, work together to solve the problem, and try again. Ask questions to get them thinking, rather than just telling them what should be done. Many things may surface in the process that will lead to learning.

- Perhaps a measuring cup cannot be found and it is needed for the next step, you could ask how we might proceed in the future so this problem would not come up again. (If everyone using the kitchen always put each item back in its proper place then it would always be available to everyone in the future! (There is a biblical truth, that just "came up" but it came with a significant meaning and may become a personal pattern.)

- Another simple, yet profound biblical truth could be taught here. God asks for the first fruits of all we earn or do. As we bake, a few extra items could be put on the cookie sheet, to give away to someone who would be blessed by them.

- At the end of the session, the kitchen should look as it did before you began. It is, after all, a public place where anyone in the family can function, so we each must clean up so it is available to the next person coming along.

You can see, perhaps, that even though the activity was done in fun, it can be used in many ways to teach important lessons. Many such opportunities can come out of a variety of interests, such as painting, drawing, skipping, running, skating, rug hooking, pottery making, kite flying, swimming, hiking, bike riding, gardening, tobogganing, raising pets, tending a bird feeder, playing an instrument. etc…etc…etc…

If you show some excitement about learning new things, your children will develop the same attitude!

This next section is not quite so easy, but it will help you understand why working with your own children is so important. It will show you that there are actually 4 different ways people learn. If you have 4 children, they may all have a different way of processing information. To complicate this even more, I have to tell you that any one person may fit anywhere on the spectrum. Each of them may be a different one of the 4 types, or some may be a blend of two, or even all four of them. I was surprised to learn that I was near the centre and a blend of all four groups!

THE LEARNING STYLES

There are many theories about learning, but this one, in my view, provides the most practical and clear message about how different people learn in different ways. It may help you understand how each of your children learn. Dr. Bernice McCarthy showed that everyone learns somewhere on a continuum between abstract thinking and feeling. She also showed that everyone learns somewhere on a continuum between observing and doing. She placed these two modes at right angles to form a cross and showed that they divided the population approximately into 4 groups. At the centre of the cross cluster the people who are more or less comfortable in all 4 groups, but at the extremities, are those who have strong preferences for one type of learning. It is possible with much planning to teach towards each group. This will be outlined briefly below under the heading "The Practice" where each group is numbered. Notice, that in the next sequence I am beginning with a description of group 2 since this is the area where most people think teaching/learning occurs.

Group 2

This group prefers observation and thinking, and is the one that learns best by reading and listening to lectures. It is the group that the church reaches best through a group presentation, explaining what the scriptures say. It is this group that can hear and benefit most from preaching. It is the mode most often used in presenting the Gospel and ministry from a pulpit. The question they want answered most often is "What...?" They want to have all the answers to the questions written down and labeled. Unfortunately, only about ¼ of the population are in this group! Similarly these people can read and grasp the text of a physics book fairly readily. The book will tell them how an electric circuit works

Group 3

This group learns best when doing and abstract thinking are linked. They need to see the practical benefit of what they are learning. This group needs to be convinced that prayer really does bring about changes. Their most favourite question would be, "How will it work...?" They need to actually pray and see God answer, while group 2 above, will be content to know it could happen. One could present the most perfect theoretical treatise on prayer but if it is not illustrated with definite authenticated examples of it working, this group would not be convinced. Even then, they will still need to see its effectiveness when they engage in it. These learners want to connect a cell, and wire to a bulb and observe that the filament glows. They will look for a way to use this concept to set up a night-light for their bedroom.

The other two groups, often present the greatest teaching challenge. They do not obtain their most important input from the written word but from their own experience. They learn best when their emotions are involved and when they are being affected by what is around them. Probably these groups are being reached best through participation in music and drama, or the on-going life of the home. Both of these groups need special teaching to enable them to connect what they feel with the truth of scripture. This is a significant challenge that is not clearly understood. Our feelings and the events around us can easily be misinterpreted. The world around us encourages us, "If it feels good, do it!" Scripture, however, reminds us that the heart is deceitful above all things and desperately wicked." The devil himself can appear as an angel of light to give us wrong direction. So these two groups need careful and earnest teaching if they are to remain true to God's word.

Group 4

This group learns best by doing and feeling. They need to be involved in doing something that gives them good feelings. They learn by trial and error. They don't primarily go to scripture and try to follow it, but try something on their own and see if it fits. These folks easily run counter to the establishment as set down in scripture, are often criticized and feel unable to contribute. Basically they learn by asking, "What will happen if I do...?" These folks need to be given lots of ideas that are known to be effective in communicating the Gospel and in serving in the church. If they try these and have success, they will learn a great deal. You can give this group a wire, bulb and electric cell, but don't bother to give them the instructions. They need to "play around" with the parts and figure out how to make the bulb glow. They would like to make a model of a bedroom, and use the circuit to light the model.

Group 1

This group learns best by reflecting on what they have experienced. As in the case of the last group, they need special help to learn how to "reflect" in a way that is consistent with scripture. They learn best when there are personal connections formed and they obtain clear understanding consistent with scripture about what is going on in their own lives. Their favorite question is, "Why?" They need to connect to real people who have had similar experiences and who have been able to explain them in the light of scripture. They need to hear of many godly saints who have analyzed their situation and have had success in understanding God's heart. They need to feel the love of the saints in the church ministering to them in tangible ways – the hands of Christ reaching out- nurturing, securing, befriending and demonstrating the commands of Christ. These learners want to know why the bulb lights up.

THE PRACTICE

Classroom teachers, who deal with all four of these learning styles at all times, are encouraged to try and connect with all students in each lesson! It can be a daunting task, but it can be done, if care is taken. A lesson that can impact all learners begins with the needs of Group one learners and progresses through the other groups in order.

The lesson would have four phases

1. Experiencing,   (What was my experience?)
2. Conceptualizing,   (What does it mean?)
3. Applying, (What does it mean to me in a practical sense?)
4. Creating. (What I am I going to do about it today?)

You can begin each lesson by drawing students through their own experiences.

A. (What have they been told, read, or seen in their past?)
B. (How do those experiences relate to the topic at hand?)
    (Move then to the second part and ask them what they consider to be the answer based on their own value system and then have them consider how that compares to what God has said.)

C. (What does this mean to me in a practical sense")
D. (What am I going to do about it today?")

Please note that every learner will not relate the same to every part, but there will be food for thought for every learner in the sequence. Each learner is drawing on his or her own experiences and personal knowledge and research to arrive at a thoughtful position. While the amount of material "covered" may seem small, it will have more significant value to each of them.

Much more detail is available on line if you care to examine it. Dr. Bernice McCarthy has a website that may be helpful. She advocates teaching classes by providing for all four groups. Her programme is called 4MAT. This information was developed by Dr. Bernice McCarthy and is used here, with her permission. It can be found on her web site:

www.aboutlearning.com/whatis4mat.

Dr. McCarthy provides a questionnaire that is used to place people on her chart to show where they fit. The chart is a circle which is divided into 4 segments by two lines – one crosses the circle horizontally, and the other crosses it vertically. Each person fits as a dot somewhere on the circle and usually in one of the 4 segments. I say, usually, because someone could actually sit on one of the lines between two segments. If that happens then they are actually able to process learning to some extent in both areas.

In the outline below, a person who is identified as at position "1" would be exclusively in Group ONE. A person at position "2" would be equally in groups ONE and FOUR, but a person identified to be in position "3" would be close to all four segments and would function more or less in all four groups. Keep this in mind while you work through the distinctive nature of the four groups.

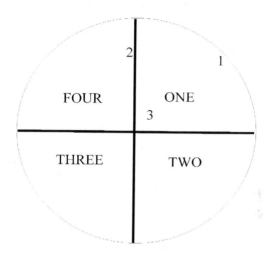

This is how educators could identify the learning preferences of your children. It is too time-consuming for most public systems, but you may find this worth doing. It may prove to you that you actually do know your children best!

Chapter Seven

BEGINNING STEPS

Congratulations on getting this far! You have waded through some deep water. I have tried to show you God's wishes for your family. We have examined some theories about learning, and tried to show you that because you know your children best, you are the best to teach them what God wills. Ultimately, He knows your children best! He has already laid out a pathway of success for each of them. Our opportunity will help the family find the knowledge and skills that will enable them to follow God's leading.

You obviously believe you want to do what God has shown you is the right thing. You are almost ready to hang out the sign, "Quiet – School in Session"

During the period when I was writing this, a major thunderstorm shook our neighbourhood one night. When I awoke I saw the grounds covered in debris. After about 4 hours of hard labour, I stopped for a rest. The Lord seemed to tell me that I should remind you that life is like that. Storms do come, and some of us have had to endure the fall-out from a list of family storms. They say that if one is raised in a dysfunctional family, they will probably develop one of their own. As I was sawing and raking up my yard, I realized that many readers may have collected negative past issues. It is important that you do whatever you can so as to minimize its affect on your children. There are steps that can be taken. The first is to ask God to reveal issues that He would have you deal with. If you are earnest about this, God will respond. He may bring events and people to your mind. If any of them need to be attended, ask God for His direction. It is important that you clear away issues that provide you with fear, or the inability to move forward. Anything that is hampering your relationship with God should be brought to Him in prayer. Be sure to renounce any past issues that were placed between you and God, so you can have an open dialogue with Him. Then give Him freedom to direct your future. If you begin to teach with a good relationship between you and the Creator, Who loves you, your children will flourish.

"How to Teach" is tightly tied to "What to Teach"! Depending on your focus at any one time, your method may change. So let's look at some ideas.

BUILD LESSONS WITHIN THEMES

(...that interest your children)

This very important part is often missed in the classroom, and yet it deals with big issues for most learners. It is the overall theme that will tie all the pieces together so that they will form an integrated whole. Most students will find it much easier to learn when all the pieces fit together to make a whole picture. The theme a parent can choose will be much more manageable for a small family group than for a whole class or school district. A family theme could be physical wellness. Under this umbrella, the children could study the biology of the human body, including its parts and their functions, the nervous system and the effects of worry and stress, nutrition and what each food contributes to our wellness, exercise that is good for you and what may be harmful, sleep and how it benefits the body. There are many references to all of this in scripture. What did Jesus say about it?

Another family theme could involve a family business and relate it to what scripture says about labour, management and money. There would be many opportunities for a study of aspects of mathematics, time, graphical presentations as a means of advertising, and group work to benefit the group rather than the individual.

Yet another theme could focus on home maintenance, involving the biology of growing vegetation for decorative purposes, or a garden to supply food. The various tasks about the dwelling could be studied and worked on. Different tasks could be assigned so that each could learn how to schedule time, and if money is paid for labour, the money could be used to teach good stewardship, giving, and savings principles and benefits.

Follow the flow of energy as a theme in an environmental study, where you are looking at different ecosystems, that involve, plants, herbivores, carnivores, and decomposers. The sun's energy, falling on the green leaves is used to make sugar. The energy in the sugar can be stored in the plant as starch in roots, and stems. The energy in the starch can be eaten by an herbivore to cause its growth and development, but it may be caught by a fox, that then has the energy to have a family, and chase rabbits. The rabbits also are able to run because they also get their energy from the starch in the plants they eat. The waste from the carnivore and the herbivore, and from dead leaves is captured by decomposers, that also use some of the sun's energy for life. Eventually, all the energy is given back in heat from all the chemistry of decomposition.

BUILD LESSONS INVOLVING SPECIAL INTERESTS

If your child loves art, work it into much of what they do and allow them to illustrate what they are learning. If your child focuses on the practicality of science, focus on the electricity that is used every day and help him or her to understand how a circuit works. If your children are focussed on print, allow them to express their feelings and successes by keeping a journal. Each learning style has a favourite way to express thought.

DEMONSTRATE SOMETHING "NEW" TO THEM.

For example, (Practice first.) cut a piece of card into a circle or square large enough to cover a class tumbler. While they are watching, fill the tumbler to the brim, place the card on top so there are no bubbles and holding it gently in place, turn the full tumbler upside down. (It might be a good idea to let your child try this with the whole thing over the kitchen sink.)

Simply ask them, "What do you think is going on here?" Let them try various alternatives, but don't be in a hurry to give them the "text-book answer"! It would be best if you are able to test the validity of their answers by experimenting with them.

GIVE THEM A WEEK TO PONDER, IF NECESSARY.

TEACH PHYSICAL SCIENCE

Don't be satisfied to teach only the biological world to your children. They will undoubtedly like to hear about the wonders of God's creation of animals and even plants, but they need to know about the rest of it. Introduce them to the physical world as well. In Physics, your children will learn of the forces in nature. Some of the early work in this field was done by a godly man who studied, not only the scriptures, but also God's creation. He became known as Sir

Isaac Newton because of what he discovered. He lived between 1642 and 1727, and wrote out the "Laws of Motion" that we still use today.

He put into words, some of what every child can learn in a playpen. His first law states that (in a child's words) my toy train will not move unless I either push it or pull it. That is one of the basics that God built into the whole of the universe. The interesting thing about this basic 'law' is that it is the same for everyone, everywhere! It doesn't change when you get older, nor does it depend on whether you are big or small, or where you were born. Everything God made is the same for everyone.

The "push" can come in many forms, by leaning against it, kicking it, or hitting it with something that will move it. Later on, the push could be applied by a windup spring or an electric motor. The push is easily illustrated in many forms of play. The child will want to be "pushed" to enjoy a ride on a swing, or to get the toboggan started on the top of a snow hill. Put your action into words so that the child will learn the concept of "forcing" an object to move. The push or the pull is an application of FORCE. This can lead to a later study.

It is important to see that there are two great reasons for you and your children to understand God's physical laws. All of the laws of physics will have the same two messages, and they are critically important.

God is "no respector of persons" – Everyone is treated alike!

As a result, the spiritual things God built into the scriptures, are the same for everyone! When God states, "You must be born again." He is saying this to everyone, with no exclusions. No one is left to wonder if it means them. It doesn't matter what age you are, or the colour of your skin, or the length of your nose or where you were born, or whether you are happy or sad! If you want to take God's offer of eternal life and be part of His forever family, you must be born anew. There must be a specific time when that birth occurred. If someone says, "I think I am part of God's family," I would question whether they have ever really known God as His child. This new birth is dramatic and it results in an about face with new desires. One important sign given is that people who know they have been adopted by God, will tell others and invite them as well.

Science can tell us many wonderful things about God's creation. Basically, it tells us what our world is like. However, it cannot tell us how or why it came to be the way it is, or even how important forces like gravity keep operating! Science can only tell us what it has seen and recorded. Knowing God is far more important than knowing science.

HEAT AND LIGHT

These are two different forms of energy. One of the great "Laws" of science states that energy cannot be created or destroyed. It can only be changed from one type to another. For example, the chemical energy stored in a cell (or battery of cells) can be changed into motion to drive a fan. It could also be changed into electric current to light a flashlight. However, every time it is used some of the energy is lost and not recoverable. It is the same with a ride on a garden swing. Someone can give you energy with a push. The swing will start off well, but will gradually slow down and stop when all the energy is used up.

There is one important thing I have noticed. People. don't seem to blame God when they fall off a roof and break a leg, or when the swing slows and stops. They seldom object to the reality of the physical laws. They accept the fact that it is harder work pedaling a bicycle up a hill. Why then do they object when God tells them that He requires them to accept His free offer of eternal life by accepting His plan for their life? It may be a puzzle that you could present to your children.

USING QUESTIONS

Jesus is the master teacher. So let us follow His example. He often began a lesson with a question. He also sometimes answered a question He was asked, by responding with His own question. He did this to encourage His students, or His enquirers to begin using their own brains – to start thinking. Earlier I pointed out that "telling" was not the same as "teaching". Telling depends on where the teller's thoughts are rather than the student's. By starting with a question we allow the student to begin thinking about and expressing where he or she is. The response can be used in more than one way. It lets the teacher understand where the student's mind is focussed. If the student is thinking in a different direction than the teacher, it would be possible to discuss how to get the two minds together on the same "page". The teacher's question may be asked to determine how much is known about the topic by the student, so the teacher can choose what "lesson" would be most effective.

A good "Rule of Thumb" is simply that the less the teacher talks, the more a student learns. If a teacher talks about an issue or topic for 20 minutes, the student's mind could be miles away and totally unconnected. It the student talks about the same topic, something has been learned, and if the teacher has been listening, a next lesson thrust has already presented itself.

<u>One Caution-</u> Your student may try to give you the answer that s/he thinks you want to hear! Their first attempt will not register as anything other than pleasing you. It is important, then, to use questions that will force them into their own thinking mode.

Let them know that you care about what they think. Encourage them to "spill out their thoughts" because you really want to know who they are! Do not be in a great hurry to correct their answers. It may be better to follow up answers with more questions. Few young people actually think they are important enough to be heard or even listened to. You can change that attitude. It will result in great benefits.

Good Questions, then, stimulate thought, and set the starting point for the next phase of learning, or establish the need to review something that may need to be re-taught or reinforced. By careful attention to the answer a teacher can determine what process of learning works best for the **student.**

What then are the characteristics of a "good question"?

A good question will give an opportunity for someone to think. A question that can be answered by "yes" or "no", would not normally cause someone to think deeply, or give the listener any clue into the thinking of the one asked. Asking, "Do you like this kind of weather?" could be answered by, "No!" A better question would be, "What kind of weather do you like the most?" The answer may be followed with, "Why do you prefer that?" Out of this type of questioning, a listener could learn more about the student.

A good question could capture the student's attention and curiosity, stimulate a desire to learn, and stimulate a series of further questions leading to more learning. It is in the student's and teacher's best interest to develop good questions.

THE WHY? QUESTION

The most often asked questions begin with who, what, where, when, and how. The answers to these lead to the most important question of all. When you ask a question beginning with the word why, you receive a different type of answer.

Many onlookers at an event, can answer the what, when, who where and how questions, but only the person who actually did the thing is able to tell why they did it! The first chapter of the Bible tells us the who, what, when and how of creation. Only the Maker can tell us why He did it. If you examine Genesis 1, you can read that God was the only person, along with His Son and His Spirit that existed, and He made everything else by thinking out its design and speaking it into existence. The rest of this amazing "love letter" tells us why He did it!

If we spend all our time asking all the simple questions about who, what, when, and how, and we never get to asking, "Why?" then we are about as wise as a creature who might prefer to live in an empty house for its life-span rather than investigate the wonders of the larger world it could enjoy.

Most of our schooling relates to the first 5 questions. Science courses teach about how things are and how they work together. It has formulas that enable us to use the force of gravity to our advantage. Science has been able to copy electric sparks and control currents to do our bidding. It has made it possible for us to light tiny fires in our homes to keep us warm. It has made it possible for us to control tiny explosions in our engines to take us travelling in our cars. It has even made it possible for us to talk to friends in other parts of the world as if they were right beside us. But—science does not answer the big question – "WHY"? In fact, we should not expect it to. It is not designed to do so, anymore than a Polar Bear is designed to fly!

Let's explore gravity. Science states that every object has a physical attraction to every other object. The amount of attraction has been measured many times. It depends on the mass of the objects and how far they are away from each other. It is important that it works this way. If it didn't we could all "fly" off into space along with, but separated from, our tricycles, cars, and houses. No scientist has been able to explain "why" this happens The fact is clear. God made our world like this because He knew it was necessary.

In the book of "Colossians" we are told that "All things were made by Jesus Christ and that by Him all things consist (are held together)." In other words, He is holding everything together by His own energy and exerting the forces necessary for us and our universe to work the way it does.

The force of gravity is like our God! It treats everyone alike. It is no respector of persons. It treats old men and babies alike. It does not depend on sex, nationality, or age! Also, it is beyond our ability to understand even how it works!

THE CHALLENGE!

This is my favourite way to teach. Whenever it fits I try to use it. The purpose is to challenge every student to perform to the best of his or her ability. Even though the children are all different and have different abilities, it is fun to watch them all succeed. In this example I can take a class of 30 children and give them each a challenge to work out on their own so that they all win! There are many ways this technique can be used. Let me share it with you.

Somewhere about Grade 4 or 5, I have given out to each student a small flashlight bulb, a small electrical cell (most people call them batteries) and one piece of wire about 6 inches long. I ask the children to find a private space in the classroom and using all three parts, light their bulb. They are not to talk to anyone or show anyone if they are successful. Instead, they are to come to me at the front of the classroom and demonstrate their success to me privately.

Each pupil takes the task seriously, and within a very short time one student will arrive to show me the lighted bulb. There is no big announcement but instead I hand that student a card that challenges the student to perform a more difficult task. It might be to add a bulb and light them both. (I always have a series of "next step" tasks for whoever is ready.) These tasks are designed to take each student a step further in the study. With the added tasks there is often added equipment. I might have a successful student go off with a second cell, and see if the two cells can make a difference to the appearance of the bulb.

In the course of about 30 minutes almost all students have not only lighted one bulb but some have done two or three different tasks such as connected two batteries in series and two in parallel, or done the same with bulbs in series or parallel. Near the end of the class, if there are two or three frustrated students who have not succeeded, I climb under the table, if necessary, with them and through questioning, walk with them until they find the necessary clue. At the end EVERYONE HAS LIT THE BULB! The point is that all are able to operate at their own speed and ability, and all feel elated! That is the beauty of what is often called "Hands-on Science".

P.S. I used the word cell above, which is correct. A "battery" is actually a group of cells connected together. Cells can be joined in parallel (beside each other) or in series (in line) to form batteries.

Here are a couple of other challenges, but you will be able to think up lots more.

ECOLOGY

In introducing groups of children to the outdoor ecosystems, I have often explained to them that every ecosystem has 4 main parts. It doesn't matter whether they are studying a metre square of lawn in front of the school or a collection of creatures from the pond. My challenge is for each child to bring me <u>evidence</u> of the four parts. (The Parts are green plants, herbivores, carnivores, & decomposers.) They don't need to bring me a grasshopper, since I only asked for "evidence". A green leaf that had a bite out of it would be evidence of an herbivore. (BUT don't tell them that! Let someone else figure it out and share it with their class!) I have seen children who were considered to be at the "bottom" of the class academically, absolutely SHINE in cases like this! A student who feels trapped in a classroom can suddenly become a leader outdoors.

ASTRONOMY

If you are doing a unit on the solar system, take your class outside at the beginning of the day (when there is a full sun shining), where there is a flagpole in some open space. Have the students stand by the shadow of the top of the pole. Ask them to go and stand where they think the shadow will be at noon. If they argue about the location, have each student or each group (if some can agree) identify the spot. You can bring along coloured paper and markers. They may need to have small flags to stick into the ground or perhaps stones to weight down the coloured paper with their names on it. When each has identified their location, ask them to also determine and mark where they think the shadow of the top of the pole will be at the end of school. Mark this as well. Your students will be anxious to check their guesses, and will learn a great deal about the path of the sun without even looking at it! (Which they must never do!) They will be anxious to share their discoveries.

You could ask them if the shadow actually fell on the spot they thought it would. Ask them, further, if they have figured out why it did or did not. Ask them what they used to make their first guess. Ask them if they now have a "new theory." Ask them to write down their theory so others could guess more accurately. These activities force a student to think and make assessments. These are valuable processes. They are the kinds of activities that cause learning to occur. One learns best by doing and thinking, not by listening and regurgitating facts. In adult life, decisions need to be made on a daily basis. Let's help our children prepare their minds to do that well.

✦— *Annotated Bibliography* —✦

I have included a few books that I have found helpful. They are not about teaching, but they offer insights into the working of a family that make teaching easy and pleasant.

"Experiencing God at Home" by Tom & Richard Blackaby would go far to set the stage for teaching your children. It was written by two men, Tom and Richard, who grew up in the Blackaby home under the direction of their famous father Henry T. Blackaby, whose book "Experiencing God" and ministry has touched many thousands around the world.

"66 Love Letters" Is a powerful overview of God's message to all of us. Dr. Larry Crabb skillfully outlines each book of the Bible in about 4 pages. He traces the clear message of God's love to each of us portrayed in every one of the 66 Books of God's Word. This is a wonderful message that shows us how we may begin to understand God's heart for us.

"Always Daddy's Girl" by Dr. H. Norman Wright, hit me with a shock about the time my oldest girl turned 20. Wright, a psychologist, explained clearly that the impact a father has on his daughter's life is extremely significant! I was stunned to find out that my girls saw me, their nearest male, as their image of what a man should be! Such an idea had never crossed my mind. They compared every male figure they saw to me. They even used me to assess the men who would woo them and marry them. It was the scariest thing I had faced. I wondered why no one had warned me. I bring it here so that any fathers who read it may come to realize the role they play in their family is huge! Play your part wisely, and enjoy its blessings!

"Love and Respect", and **"Love and Respect in the Family"** are two books by Dr. Emerson Eggeriches, and his daughter, highlighting a major issue that often goes a long way towards destroying families. They show that men and women were made to complement each other, by being different in their make-up. This difference shows up, of course, in families where boys and girls are trying to get along together as well as mother and father. God's Word says that men should love their wives and that wives should respect their husbands, but it doesn't explain that God made each of them in such a way that they actually respond best to what He has told us to do! We tend to think, naturally, (and the evil one helps us get it all wrong) that one needs to show a good reason before I can treat them the way God expects. The fact is that they will respond the way I want <u>when I</u> do what God tells <u>me to do</u>! Understanding this one simple idea can bring harmony to the family, and make teaching a pleasure.

This next book set can make a huge difference to our understanding of boys and girls, and their need for both Mom and Dad!

Wild At Heart" by John Eldredge, -identifies 5 stages a boy goes through to become a fully functional man. He points out that missing even one of the stages can seriously hamper God's vision for a man's future. He makes it clear that the father of the boy is an essential part of his development. Without a father and a mother functioning God's way, the boy will struggle with who he is, and what role he will be able to play.

"Captivating" by John & Stasi Eldredge follows the same plan but focuses on the development of a girl through 5 stages to become the woman God intended her to be. This book clearly shows both the mother's and the father's roles in the development of the girl becoming a woman.

These books are also favourites, but they have a different value. These are resources that can help us grow spiritually.

"Lessons From A Sheep Dog" by Phillip Keller
This is a delightful book that your children might enjoy. It tells a true story of Phillip's rescue of a damaged dog that he loved and cared for until he was able to "win" it's trust and become his valued team-mate. A beautiful example of how our Lord looks for us, finds us, wins our trust, and then invests in us so He can use us for His service.

"Mastering Life" by Robert J. Morgan
He presents 10 biblical strategies that can bring us to a lifetime of purpose. This would be a great resource when presenting to your children ways of bringing life under control as God would have us. He describes time management, orderliness, planning, and 7 other things that God has laid out in the Bible, for our success

"The Greatest Words Ever Spoken" - compiled by Steven K. Scott.
This is a presentation of all the "red-letter" words of Jesus, classified under more than 200 different topics. It is an impressive resource, where you can find everything Jesus said about the 200 topics

THREE BOOKS BY JOSH MCDOWELL

"More Than A Carpenter" provides a basic picture of Who Jesus is, and it ends with Josh's personal story of how, as a child, he was abused and hated God. In trying to prove there was no God, he traveled to Europe and God met him there. Josh now travels the world, preaching and teaching through sermons, debates and through his many books.

"Undaunted" is his autobiography. He tells how he, a farm boy in a dysfunctional family was abused and became so bitter that he determined to find a way to destroy Christianity! He traveled to Europe and investigated many of the original writings to find a way to disprove Jesus' resurrection! He found out, instead, that it was all true! He became a believer and has traveled the world speaking eloquently about Christ

"Evidence That Demands A Verdict" is a great resource. It provides hundreds of proofs that God is real. It clarifies, for all those who need it, that the scriptures could not have been written by anyone except God Himself!

An AFTER-WORD ...For Fathers

This book grew out of a small pamphlet I produced about 10 years ago for fathers. I was concerned, then, for the lack of involvement by fathers for their children. The situation has worsened since, and some have stated that up to 50% of our children to-day, have either no father in the home or one who has shown no leadership in the development of their children.

It is obvious from scripture that fathers were expected to take a leadership role in the family. The evil one is trying to destroy our children. There is a need for dad to take charge, not with his personal power, or authority – but by allowing God to work through him so everyone will be successful and fulfilled. I began this whole writing venture with the following message.

The call, "Gentlemen, start your engines!" begins one of the world's great auto races. It follows years of preparation and practice and focuses on the glory of success. The sophisticated equipment involved and the techniques employed have evolved from simple beginnings. If you are a man who bears Christ's name you are participating in an even greater race which has even greater rewards! We are on the last lap and have a great deal of "catching up" to do, but we have the means to win!

The supporting structures are all in place. You are not required to design a car or organize a pit crew. You are equipped to take control and steer to the finish line. Without you, the rest of the team's efforts are wasted!

Your instructions for success in the race of life are clearly given and all necessary support is provided. God, Who created the universe, has a plan for you to win your race if you want to. If you decide not to play your part, the prize will be lost. Your family, and all those who look up to you for direction, will be affected as well.

Your response may be anywhere from: "I know these issues and have them well under control with those around me" to: "I'm not a teacher and I'm unable to do this!"

To the first I say you need to help those around you to come to your understanding. There are many that need your expertise. To the second, I say there are two realities that make it clear you **should** and that you **can** teach. You should because Jesus commanded it and it is of critical importance to those around you. You can teach because Jesus would not have commanded it if He knew you couldn't.

Hanani, the seer, told Asa, the king of Judah, that "the eyes of the LORD run to and fro throughout the whole earth, to show Himself strong in the behalf of them whose heart is perfect toward him." (2 Chron. 16:9). In other words, if we are doing what God wants, He will give us what we need. Regardless of your past successes or failures, God is waiting and watching for you to whole-heartedly agree to serve Him. He will support you! He wants to bless you!

We should be like Jabez. (1 Chron. 4:9,10) He was "more honourable than his brethren" because of his prayer, for he called upon his God to bless him, to enlarge his witness, to keep His hand on him, and to keep him from evil. God granted him his request!

I don't believe there has ever been a more important job for fathers to tackle. Your children, and those who live about you, need to be taught God's Word and you can learn to do it effectively. You should begin immediately. It is easier if your children are young. It becomes increasingly more difficult if they have already reached their teen years.

If you agree this is an urgent matter, and would like to discuss this further, I would try to help.

Contact me at teachyourchildren.online

Printed in the United States
By Bookmasters